THE QUICK GUIDE TO
Taking
in a Lodger

Tessa Shepperson

Lawpack Publishing Limited
76–89 Alscot Road
London SE1 3AW

www.lawpack.co.uk

ISBN: 9781906971199
E-book ISBN: 9781906971434

First published 2010; reprinted 2011, 2012

The law is stated as at 1 February 2012.

MIX
Paper from
responsible sources
FSC® C011748

Exclusion of liability and disclaimer

Contents

Introduction

If you have a house or a flat with a spare room, you have an instant way to earn a bit of extra cash. Why not rent a room to a lodger? This is what I did for about six years in the 1990s. After buying my house in 1989 I found balancing my finances particularly difficult. As a trainee solicitor my salary was modest, and the building work needed on the house had proved more expensive than I had anticipated. So I contacted the accommodation office of my local university and started taking in students.

Initially most of the students were mature foreign students on short courses, mostly learning English. The accommodation was well paid as I also provided meals (part of the job was to talk to them over supper), and I met some delightful people. In particular, there was Maria from Valencia who took me out for a meal on her last night; and Gisina, a trainee doctor from East Germany who loved gardening and helped me on my allotment. Then there was Maria from the Caribbean who had such a wonderful sense of humour and who insisted on helping with the washing up; sweet Carla from the mountains of Switzerland; and numerous Austrian lady teachers on regular three-week English teaching courses.

The students (those on the courses anyway) had all been told to give their landlady a present, which is why I now have a decorative plate from Zaragoza, a painted tray from Turkey and some heart-shaped earrings from Brazil. However, the Mozart chocolate and marzipan sweets (a popular present from my Austrian students) are long gone, along with the bottle of genuine Caribbean rum.

Presents notwithstanding, it was fascinating to talk to so many people from other countries and get an understanding of their culture. As well as my visitors' book, I also kept a recipe book and still use some of the recipes that were given to me.

In later years, numbers from courses dwindled so I started taking in local students. Most of these stayed for the whole year. They were surprisingly unobtrusive and no trouble at all. All of them paid in cash every Saturday without fail. My favourite was Sheldon who was doing a course in film studies. Film was his passion; he was invariably late for everything, but somehow always managed to be there for the start of Barry Norman's television film programme! I often wondered what happened to him. Then the HR office at work learned that I took in lodgers and started asking me if I could put up new members of staff for a few weeks while they found somewhere permanent to live. I only stopped taking in lodgers after I married late in 1995.

Of course it was not all straightforward. There was the ultra-fussy student from Spain who would not eat anything (most students loved my cooking) and the young man from South America who expected me to wait on him hand and foot (not my style). There was the Muslim Turkish student who told me that he would 'eat everything', only to amend this later (after I served him pork casserole) saying that it never occurred to him that anyone actually ate pork! Then there was the Japanese girl who sent her luggage on ahead of her by parcel post only to find that her (enormous) suitcase had been damaged in transit. However, these were only minor problems.

I can honestly say that the overwhelming majority of my lodgers were utterly charming and delightful, and the experience of having them to stay has enriched my life.

This book comes partly from that experience. It also comes from my experience as a solicitor specialising in landlord and tenant law, including advising landlords with lodgers. So most of this book is written from a lawyer's perspective, advising you on the legal obligations which you will take on if you decide to let to lodgers.

The book is also a companion to the Lawpack products for lodger landlords, in particular the *Lodger Agreement: For a Room in a Furnished House or Flat with a Resident Owner* and the *Property Inventory*. You will also find a certain amount of information on my website service, www.lodgerlandlord.co.uk.

CHAPTER 1
What is a lodger?

Generally when we say 'lodger' we mean someone who rents a bedroom in his landlord's home. The lodger will generally be given a key to the front door, and will share the bathroom, kitchen and living room with the landlord and his family. The landlord will often provide clean sheets and towels on a weekly or fortnightly basis, and sometimes will also provide cleaning services and meals. It depends very much on what the lodger wants and what the landlord is prepared to provide.

Note that this book only looks at lodgers. It does not cover au pairs and live-in nannies, as they are employees and you will need to consider employment law issues. For more information on this, see Lawpack's useful products *Employment Law Made Easy* by Melanie Slocombe and *Employment Contracts Kit*.

Many people also often take in short-term visitors on holidays as paying guests. Most of the legal rules set out in this book will also apply to paying guests such as those on holiday, but this book is for landlords where lodgers stay with you long term rather than where people stay short term as a holiday.

Tenancies and licences

'Lodger' is not a legal term. In legal language, if someone rents property he will be either a 'tenant' or a 'licensee'. There is a big legal difference between these.

Tenancies (where the tenant in effect owns the property for a period of time) carry with them a number of important legal rights and obligations which, if they are not written into the tenancy agreement, will be implied into it by law. However, this is not the case with a licence. A licence is simply permission to occupy a property so that the person occupying is not a trespasser.

The legal status of a person's occupation will normally depend on what actually happens. So if someone rents a whole house or flat (with the landlord living elsewhere) and pays rent for it, this will normally be a tenancy, and the fact that the occupier has signed an agreement saying that it is a licence agreement will not change this.

However, if someone lives somewhere with the permission of the owner, but does not have a tenancy, he will normally have a licence. This is usually because he does not rent a house, flat or room exclusively to himself, for example if he lives in a shared bedroom or dormitory in a hostel.

If you are renting out a room in your house, you will not want to create a tenancy, so you should make sure that the person you are renting to only has a licence. Most lodger situations are licences automatically, but it is as well to be aware of the difference and know how to avoid a tenancy being created (see below).

Please note that this book does not cover the law relating to tenancies, which is dealt with in my other two books, *The Complete Guide to Residential Letting* and *Renting: The Essential Guide to Tenants' Rights*, both published by Lawpack.

Important elements

This section looks at what is normally involved in renting to a lodger and what you need to avoid to prevent a tenancy being created.

The lodger will rent a room (occasionally two) in your house (or flat).

You must make it clear that you have the right to enter this room from time to time (while respecting the lodger's privacy). This is important. Do not allow a situation to develop where your lodger has a lock on the door which prevents your entering.

Generally the lodger will share some living space with his landlord. This will generally include the kitchen, bathroom and living room, or one or more of these. It is important that some living space is shared as otherwise this may affect your right to evict your lodger without a Court hearing (see more on this in chapter 8); hallways and corridors do not count.

The landlord will normally provide some services. This could be just providing clean sheets, and perhaps towels, every one or two weeks. Sometimes the landlord will provide cleaning services, and perhaps meals. It is a good idea to do this, as it is impossible for a tenancy to be created if services are provided. It is particularly important to provide some services if you are not sharing any living space, as otherwise this is likely to be a tenancy. However, please note that this book is really aimed at lodger landlords, and those will be where living space is shared.

Note: if you have a situation where you rent out one or more self-contained rooms, which have locks on the doors, to someone who shares no living accommodation with you and where you never enter the rooms or provide any services, then this will be a tenancy (where you are a resident landlord) and will not be covered in this book.

Reasons to avoid creating a tenancy:

- You will be bound by 'statutory repairing covenants' (meaning that your tenant can go to court to force you to do repair work (relating to the matters covered in the relevant statute) and claim compensation).

- You will have to obtain a court order if you need to evict your tenant.

- It will almost certainly put you in breach of your mortgage or tenancy agreement (unless you have permission).

Note also that to qualify as a resident landlord you must have lived at the property as your only or main home for the whole time the lodger has been living there. If you move into a property and take over as landlord in a situation where the lodgers are already in occupation, there may be problems and you should take legal advice. You should also remain living in the property until the lodger moves out, although temporary absences such as holidays are all right.

Summary

In this book, when we refer to a lodger this means someone who rents out a room in his landlord's house or flat but who does not have complete control over it, as the landlord retains the right to enter it from time to time. The lodger will share some living accommodation with his landlord, who will also provide one or more services such as fresh bed linen and cleaning. The landlord will be someone who was living at the property at the time the lodger moved in and who remains living in the property for the whole of the lodger's period of occupation (other than temporary absences such as holidays).

CHAPTER 2

Legal and practical considerations

Before you start looking for your lodger, there are a number of legal and practical matters you will need to sort out first.

Permissions

It is important that you check that you are allowed to take in a lodger. The main situations are listed below:

Owner-occupiers – in almost all cases there should be no problem. It is possible that if you own a long lease this may have restrictions on your taking in paying guests, but this is unlikely (although you should check). If you have a mortgage, it is also possible that there may be restrictions, but if so these will normally be against subletting rather than taking in a lodger. You should be careful therefore to make sure that your lodger does not acquire a tenancy (see chapter 1). If you take more than two lodgers it is possible that you may have to apply for planning permission or an HMO licence. If you think this will affect you, have a word with the planning officer at your local authority.

Local authority or housing association tenants – again there will not normally be any problem about taking in a lodger (although you should check with your local office first), but you should not allow the lodger to acquire a tenancy.

Private tenants – most tenancy agreements will have a clause forbidding any sharing of the property or subletting. You will therefore need to get your landlord's permission before taking in a lodger. However, if the main reason for your taking in a lodger is to help you pay your rent, most landlords will be happy with this! There is no need to get your tenancy agreement amended. A letter from your landlord confirming that he does not object to your having a lodger will be sufficient. Keep this letter safe with your tenancy agreement. Again, you must be careful to ensure that your lodger does not acquire a tenancy.

Many people take in lodgers without even considering whether or not they ought to obtain the permissions discussed above and do not have any problems. In most circumstances, even if permission is required, it will normally be granted anyway. This is because the main reason for taking in a lodger is to help pay the rent or mortgage – something your landlord or mortgage company will approve of!

However, even though in most cases there will be no objection, it is as well to check and make sure. If you let without permission in circumstances where permission would not have been granted, you may put your tenancy or mortgage at risk.

Reasons why permission may be withheld

There are two main reasons:

HMO licence conditions – if you live in a property which is classed as an HMO (for information about HMOs see chapter 3), for example if you and several friends rent a property together on an Assured Shorthold Tenancy (AST), your landlord may have had to obtain a licence from the local authority. If so, the local authority will normally have set a maximum number of people who can live in the property. If your lodger will bring the number of people over the permitted limit, then your landlord will not be able to give permission for you to take in the lodger – if he does so he will breach the terms of his licence and will risk being fined and being refused a licence in future.

Generally a landlord will need to obtain a licence if the property has three or more storeys and has five or more occupants living in two or more households. However, in some areas of the country, local authority licences will also be needed for other types of property and situation. For more information on HMOs and licences see chapter 3.

Overcrowding – if a property falls within one of the statutory definitions of overcrowding, then this will be a criminal offence. A property will be overcrowded if people of the opposite sex (other than married or cohabiting couples) have to share a bedroom, or if there are too many people for the size of the building. There are two ways of calculating this, see the tables below. Both should be applied and the one which gives the lower figure will be the statutory limit.

Calculating overcrowding

Method 1					
Number of rooms	1	2	3	4	5+
Maximum number of people	2	3	5	7½	2 per room

Method 2				
Floor area of the room in sq feet	110	90–109	70–89	50–69
Number of people	2	1½	1	½

In both cases:

• children under one year old are ignored;

• children under ten years old, but not under one, count as a half;

• rooms under 50 square feet are ignored;

- a room is counted if it is either a living room or a bedroom (a large kitchen may be held to be a living room).

Note that the room standard is also contravened when the number of persons sleeping in a property and the number of rooms available as sleeping accommodation is such that two persons of opposite sexes, who are not living together as husband and wife, must sleep in the same room.

Insurance

You need to let your insurers know that you will be taking a lodger and you should not go ahead until they have confirmed that they have no objection. Otherwise they may be entitled to refuse to pay out if you need to make a claim. Below is an example of a letter to send to your insurance company. It is also a good idea to take out third-party liability insurance against possible claims by lodgers for injury as a result of defects in your property or its contents. However, this will involve additional expense.

Bear in mind also that many insurers will only pay out on a claim for theft if entry to the property was forced. This will not be the case if the thief was your lodger, as he would be in the property with your permission, and will probably have a key. It is unlikely, therefore, that your insurance will cover damage to or theft of your contents by a lodger or paying guest. It is also unlikely that your insurers will extend the third-party public liability cover to include damage or injury caused by the lodger, although there should be no problem getting cover extended to include injury, etc. to the lodger caused by your negligence. However, you need to check this.

Another important point is that insurers will often expect you to check whether your lodger has any criminal convictions, and will refuse to pay claims if it turns out that they do. You should therefore put this question on your application form – the fact that it is there and that you have required your lodger to answer it will normally satisfy the insurance company. Note that if you want to take in a lodger who has a past conviction (after all they have to live somewhere!) the charity Unlock will be able to find you an insurance company who can help. They have a website at www.unlock.org.uk.

Note that this book can only give very general guidance on insurance matters. If you want further information, you should speak to an insurance broker or independent financial adviser.

Letter to insurance company template

[Your address]

To: [Insurer's name and address]

Date:

Dear Sirs

[Head the letter with your insurance policy number and address]

I am writing to inform you that I am considering taking in a lodger at my property.

Can you please confirm that my property/contents insurance will remain in force during the letting and let me know what the position is under my policy for the following:

- Damage to my property/contents by my lodger and/or my lodger's visitors.
- Theft of contents by my lodger and/or my lodger's visitors.
- Injury or death of my lodger and/or my lodger's visitors.
- Damage to my lodger's belongings caused by defects in my property/contents.

Please also confirm that I have third-party liability cover which will extend to my lodger and my lodger's visitors.

I look forward to hearing from you as soon as possible.

Yours faithfully

[Your name and signature]

Gas safety

Gas can be very dangerous and there have been quite a few cases where people (generally tenants) have died because gas appliances have not been properly maintained. It is for this reason that there are regulations to ensure that these appliances are regularly checked if a property is rented out to tenants or rooms to paying guests.

The Gas Safety Regulations provide that landlords must arrange for gas appliances to be inspected before the property is rented out or the paying guests arrive, and then be inspected every year, by a gas installer registered with the Gas Safe Register, and a certificate obtained from the installer. Failure to do this is a criminal offence.

If you are a tenant in a property, your landlord should have provided you with a copy of the certificate. If this has not been done, you should contact your landlord and ask for it. If he refuses, you can complain to your local Health and Safety Executive (HSE), who enforce the gas regulations.

If you own your property, then you have to obtain the certificate. There are lots of companies that do this work, and they will often say in their advertisements (e.g. in the Yellow Pages) that they provide gas certificates for landlords. It is important that the supplier you use is registered with the Gas Safe Register, but you can check this on the Gas Safe website at www.gassaferegister.co.uk or telephone 0800 408 5500.

You will find more information about gas safety and the role of the HSE on their website at www.hse.gov.uk – follow the links for 'Gas'.

Warning signs to watch out for with gas appliances:

- Dust and detritus in a gas appliance can cause it to become unsafe. A sign of this is when the colour of the flame changes to a smoky yellow.
- Black soot deposits around gas appliances.

- Cracks in the cement blocks found in older fires and mobile heaters.
- Poor ventilation, caused either by a blocked flue or by ventilation in a room (e.g. air bricks) becoming blocked, which can cause a build-up of carbon monoxide in the air.
- Gas leaks, for example if gas pipes become damaged. It is important to ensure that vulnerable pipes are protected.

Furniture and other items

All furniture and furnishings in your property (or at least the part used by the lodger) must comply with fire and furniture regulations. This means basically that the furniture must be fire-retardant and be correctly labelled. The only exceptions are items made before 1950. If you have purchased furniture recently, it should be compliant.

There are various other product safety regulations such as for electrical products, cookers, and general safety regulations which will apply. You should therefore try to ensure that all items in your property, at least all those in the lodger's room and in places where he is likely to use them, are in a safe condition.

These regulations are regulated by local authority Trading Standards Offices and they will be able to provide you with informative leaflets. These will also show the labels which need to be attached to your furniture and furnishings. Trading Standards Officers are generally friendly and keen to help, as they much prefer helping people avoid problems than prosecuting them! A visit to see them is generally well worth the effort.

You can find out details of your local Trading Standards Office via the website www.tradingstandards.gov.uk, or by ringing up your local authority main switchboard and asking them.

The condition of your property

As a landlord letting to lodgers in your own home, you are not bound by the repairing covenants set out in Section 11 of the Landlord and Tenant Act, in the same way that landlords of tenants are. However, note that all residential properties are subject to basic health and safety standards, which can be enforced by local authorities.

So, for example, if your lodger were to complain to them, a local authority Environmental Health Officer (EHO) could attend and carry out a Housing Health and Safety Rating System (HHSRS) inspection. He would check your property against a number of defined 'hazards' and at the time of writing there are 29 of these. If he found any 'category 1' (i.e. very serious) hazards, he could serve an improvement notice on you, ordering you to carry out works to bring the property up to standard. You will find a list of the 29 hazards which properties are assessed against in the table below. If you require further information, you will find a number of guides on the Communities and Local Government website at www.communities.gov.uk/housing.

In reality, it is unlikely that you will be subject to an HHSRS inspection; however, it is worth bearing in mind that these standards do exist and trying to ensure that your property is in a generally safe condition. More information on the HHSRS can be found in the Housing section of the Communities and Local Government website at www.communities.gov.uk.

The 29 HHSRS Hazards

A. Physiological requirements	B. Psychological requirements
• Damp and mould growth • Excess cold • Excess heat • Asbestos (and man-made fibres)	• Crowding and space • Entry by intruders • Lighting • Noise

• Biocides • Carbon monoxide, etc. • Lead • Radiation • Un-combusted fuel gas • Volatile organic compounds	
C. Protection against infection	**D. Protection against accidents**
• Domestic hygiene, pests and refuse • Food safety • Personal hygiene, sanitation and drainage • Water supply	• Falls associated with baths • Falls on the level • Falls associated with stairs and steps • Falls between levels • Electrical hazards • Fire • Hot surfaces and materials • Collision and entrapment • Explosions • Position and operability of amenities • Structural collapse and failing elements

Adapting your property

You may be considering doing some building work, for example to create a new room in the loft, or basement or over your garage, which you can let out, or to add a new bathroom. If so, bear in mind the following:

• If you rent your home, you will need to get permission from your landlord. If you rent from a private landlord, it is most unlikely that this will be granted.

• If your property is leasehold (i.e. if your lease is for over 21 years as opposed to an AST), then you should check your lease to see if you need to get permission from your freeholder or head lessor.

- If you have a mortgage, check to see whether your mortgage company will need to know about this (although you may be doing this anyway as they will normally be the first people to speak to about finance).

- You should also check with your insurers to see if any change is needed in your policy.

- You may need planning permission for some types of work (particularly if your property is a listed building or is in an Area of Outstanding Natural Beauty) – your builder or architect should advise you.

- You will almost certainly need building regulation approval. Again, your builder or architect will advise you.

Getting help

Electrical safety – if you are not sure whether the electrical wiring in your property is safe, your electricity supplier will be able to arrange for it to be inspected free of charge. If you would like this, have a word with their customer services helpline. However, bear in mind that if there are serious problems, they will generally require remedial work to be done immediately, and they may want to cut your supply off until works have been done.

Fire safety – your local Fire Prevention Officer will be happy to advise on fire safety. This is a free service and it is a good idea to obtain a report from him even if you are not taking in lodgers.

Grants – there are various grants available, particularly if your property is substandard, or if you want to carry out energy saving improvements. Contact your local authority (for general grants) and the Energy Saving Trust (www.energysavingtrust.org.uk) or have a word with your Citizens Advice Bureau, who may have a list of grant providers in your area.

Trading Standards – although their official function is to prosecute those breaching the regulations, Trading Standards Officers consider that a major part of their work is to assist people from falling foul of the regulations in the first place, and they will be only too happy to discuss your obligations and provide helpful leaflets and guidance. They are a very good source of information. You can find your local office via the website www.tradingstandards.gov.uk.

Gas safety – as mentioned above, information can be found on the HSE website at www.hse.gov.uk and also on the Gas Safe Register website at www.gassaferegister.co.uk. To check whether an engineer is registered with them telephone 0800 408 5500.

Vermin and insect infestation – this can happen to the best of us. Rats get everywhere and if you have animals, flea infestation is very likely at some stage or other. It does not mean you are particularly dirty! Local authorities will have a free or low-cost pest control service, and your vet will be happy to advise you on getting rid of fleas on pets.

Remember, if your lodger suffers an injury because your property is not in a proper condition, you could be sued for compensation! Insurance cover can help with claims, but best to make sure the property is in a good condition in the first place.

Energy Performance Certificates (EPCs)

You may have read that there is a new obligation on landlords to provide a copy of an Energy Performance Certificate to tenants. You will be pleased to learn that this does not apply to you, as EPCs are only needed for self-contained accommodation. This is not the case with lodgers as they will be sharing part of your property with you.

However, you may want to consider getting an EPC anyway. They are not that expensive and will help identify areas where you can save energy (and therefore money!). If your property is an energy-efficient one, this will be attractive for potential lodgers as many people are concerned about climate change and the need to conserve energy.

EPCs must be produced by accredited domestic energy assessors. You can find out more about EPCs and find a domestic energy assessor near you at www.hcrregister.com.

Décor and furniture in the room

This is really up to you, provided you comply with all your legal obligations as listed above. However, neutral colours are least likely to put someone off when viewing your room. Having a decent carpet can do a lot for the appearance of a room, but make sure that the carpet you choose is a neutral colour and hard-wearing. If you are short of cash, you can often get very nice offcuts cheap in carpet warehouses.

As far as furniture and other items are concerned you should have the following:

- A decent and comfortable bed. Consider fitting a waterproof mattress cover to protect it from stains.

- A chair and desk or computer workstation, with lamp or good overhead lighting.

- A bookcase or shelves on the wall.

- Lots of storage space for clothes and other items.

- A bedside table with lamp and perhaps a clock radio.

- Some form of heating.

All electrical items should ideally be new; make sure you keep the receipts and instruction books.

Decide whether you are going to allow pictures on the wall. If you do not want to allow Blu-Tack (or similar), a picture rail (with hooks) and a pinboard/notice board may be a good idea.

Keeping records

I strongly recommend that you keep very careful records of everything. Have a place where you put all receipts and forms; for example, your gas safety certificate, receipts for furniture and other items for the lodger's room and receipts for any repair or other work done to the room, so you can always find them easily if needed. Perhaps keep a drawer in your desk (or filing cabinet if you have one) just for this. If you have a lot of paperwork, keep separate files for certificates, receipts, adverts, etc. and I would also suggest you have a separate file for each lodger.

CHAPTER 3
Houses in Multiple Occupation (HMOs)

A House in Multiple Occupation (HMO) exists where a number of people who are unrelated or do not form a single 'household' live together in a property. Examples of HMOs include houses that are bedsits, hostels, bed and breakfast accommodation, and sometimes, landlords taking lodgers into their own home. There are two circumstances where you will need to take account of the HMO legislation:

1. if you are living in a property which is already classed as an HMO; and

2. if your property becomes classed as an HMO because of the number of lodgers you have.

There are two consequences of a property being classed as an HMO:

1. the HMO Management Regulations will apply; and

2. landlords of some types of HMO may need to obtain a licence from the local authority.

It is important therefore that you know whether your property is an HMO or not. HMOs are defined in a long and complex section in the Housing Act 2004 (Section 254 onwards), but it is not generally necessary to read this.

Is your property already an HMO?

The property you live in could already be an HMO:

- if you live in a self-contained flat which was converted from a single building, then if this was done before June 1992 and two-thirds or more of the flats are let out as ASTs; or

- if you are one of several tenants, who are not related to each other, and who have signed a tenancy agreement together (e.g. if you rent your flat with two or more friends).

As discussed in chapter 2, if the property you are living in is already an HMO, it may have been necessary for your landlord to obtain a licence from the local authority. This licence will specify a maximum number of occupiers for the property. Your landlord will not be able to give you permission to take a lodger if this would bring the number of people living in the property over the permitted maximum.

Will taking in a lodger create an HMO?

A property is classed as an HMO if there are two or more households which share living accommodation. A household is generally a family unit (including parents, grandparents, children (and step-children), grandchildren, brothers, sisters, uncles, aunts, nephews, nieces or cousins), so if you take in your cousin as a lodger this will not count as a separate household. It is the same with any 'domestic staff' who live with you, for example an au pair or nanny as they are counted as part of your family.

As a live-in landlord, you are allowed two 'non-family' lodgers before your property will be classed as an HMO. Therefore if you take in three non-family lodgers your property will be an HMO. However, if you take in two uncles, your cousin and a live-in au pair, your property will not be an HMO, even though there will be more people living in it.

Note that if you have any half-relatives or foster children, these will also count as part of your household.

What about licensing?

Many people with lodgers do not realise that they may have to obtain an HMO licence from their local authority. You will normally need a licence if:

- your property is an HMO for the reasons described above; and

- the property has three or more storeys; and

- there are four or more people living at the property in addition to yourself and your family (including any family who are lodgers and any domestic staff).

To work out how many storeys there are, you need to include all actual storeys in the building including attics and basements if these have been converted to residential use or if they are used for business purposes. So if you have a standard two-storey house where the attic has been converted to a bedroom then this will count as a three-storey house.

If you are not sure whether your house or flat will come within the definition, have a word with your local authority. Generally they will have a separate department which deals with HMOs and the licensing of HMOs.

Note that in some areas local authorities have introduced additional licensing requirements, so if you have three or more lodgers (who are not family) you might want to check with them. However, if you only have two non-family lodgers you will be safe.

If you find out that your property is one that will need licensing, you will need to obtain the licence before taking in your third non-family lodger. This will involve completing a form and paying the relevant licence fee. The fee varies from local authority to local authority. In some areas it is under £100 but in others it will be over £1,000. In most (although not all) cases the licence will last for five years.

The HMO Management Regulations

Most landlords with lodgers will not need to worry about these, but as set out above, they may apply to you if you have more than three lodgers. However, if you do fall in the category of an HMO, you will be bound by the additional obligations set out in the Management of Houses in Multiple Occupation (England) Regulations 2006 whether or not you need to obtain an HMO licence. The regulations can be summarised as follows:

- **Contact details** – the landlord or person managing the HMO (referred to as 'the Manager') must ensure that his name, address and contact telephone number are made available to all occupiers and are clearly displayed in a prominent position in the property.

- **Fire safety** – the Manager must make sure that all means of escape from fire are kept free from obstruction and maintained in good order and repair. Any firefighting equipment must be kept in good working order, and (unless there are four or fewer occupiers) notices indicating the location of the means of escape from fire must be displayed in prominent positions so they are clearly visible to occupiers.

- **General safety** – the Manager must take reasonable measures to protect occupiers from injury, with regard to the design of the HMO, its structural condition, and the number of occupiers. In particular, he must ensure that roofs and balconies are safe or take measures to prevent access. Windows with low sills must have bars or other safeguards.

- **Water supply** – the water supply and drainage system must be kept in good, clean and working condition. In particular, cisterns and tanks must be covered, and fittings must be protected from frost damage. The Manager must not do anything to interfere with the supply of water or drainage.

- **Gas safety** – the gas regulations will apply as they do to all residential lettings, and the Manager must supply a copy of the latest gas certificate to the local authority within seven days of receiving a written request.

- **Electrical safety** – every electrical installation must be inspected and tested at least every five years by a qualified electrician and a certificate obtained. This must be supplied to the local authority within seven days of receipt of a written request. The Manager must not do anything to interfere with the supply of electricity.

- **The common parts** – the Manager must maintain the common parts of the HMO in good and clean decorative order, in a safe and working condition, and reasonably clear from obstruction. In particular, all handrails and banisters must be kept in good repair and additional ones added if necessary for safety; stair coverings kept securely fixed and in good repair; windows and other ventilation kept in good repair; adequate light fittings; and all fixtures, fittings and appliances used in common by occupiers must be kept in good and safe repair and in clean working order. However, this does not apply to items occupiers are entitled to remove (e.g. their own possessions). Note that 'common parts' for which the Manager has responsibility include entrance doors (including to occupiers' own rooms), stairs, passages and corridors, lobbies, entrances, balconies, porches and steps – basically the parts of the property used by occupiers to gain access to their own accommodation and any other part of the property shared by occupiers.

- **Outside areas** – outbuildings, yards and forecourts used by occupiers must be maintained in good repair, clean condition and good order, and gardens kept in a safe and tidy condition. Boundary walls, railings, fences, etc. must be kept in good and safe repair so not a danger to occupiers.

- **Unused areas** – if any part of the property is not in use, Managers need to ensure that areas that give direct access to it are kept clean and free from rubbish.

- **Living accommodation** – the Manager must ensure that living accommodation and furniture for the occupiers' own use is in a clean condition at the start of their occupation, and that the internal structure and any fixtures, fittings or appliances are maintained in good repair and clean working order, including windows. However, this does not apply to damage caused by the occupier failing to comply with the terms of his letting agreement, or if he fails to conduct himself in a reasonable manner, or to things he is entitled to remove from the property (e.g. his own possessions).

- **Rubbish disposal** – the Manager must ensure that suitable and sufficient litter bins and/or bags are provided, and to make arrangements for the disposal of rubbish in line with the local authority's collection services.

The regulations initially sound intimidating, but in fact they mostly boil down to having your property in a good and safe condition. Most of the matters set out here will be complied with anyway by responsible landlords. The only real 'new' item is the requirement to have an electrical safety check every five years and get a certificate.

Note that it is not just landlords who have obligations under these regulations. The regulations also say that occupiers must not hinder or frustrate the Manager in the execution of his duties; must allow the Manager access at reasonable times; provide the Manager with any information he may reasonably require; take care with and not damage anything the Manager is bound to maintain under the regulations; deal with rubbish as required by the landlord; and comply with any reasonable instructions from the Manager as regards fire safety.

Breach of these regulations (by either landlord or occupier) is a criminal offence punishable by a fine in the Magistrates' Court. The local authority is the main prosecuting organisation; this is not something the police will deal with. In reality they are unlikely to bring a prosecution apart from in serious cases, and only after the landlord has ignored their requests to carry out improvements to their procedures.

CHAPTER 4

Money and tax

Setting the rent

Before you start looking for a lodger you need to know how much you are going to charge him. Your level of rent needs to be similar to that set by other landlords in the area, so you will need to do a bit of investigation to find out what people are charging.

If you know someone who takes in lodgers, have a word with him, or you could make enquiries of the organisations discussed in the next chapter. Also take a look at other people's advertisements, for example in shop windows.

Deposits

You will probably want to take a deposit from your lodger. This is a sum of money held by the landlord until the lodger leaves, when it can then be used to cover the cost of making good any damage, replacing any missing items in his room, or covering any outstanding rent. Deposits are normally equivalent to one month's rent, although sometimes they are higher (e.g. you may want to take a higher deposit if you are taking in a lodger with a dog, to cover any extra damage which the dog might do).

There are a number of reasons why taking a deposit is a good idea:

- The fact that your lodger is able to afford to pay a deposit is in itself a good indication of his financial soundness.

- The risk of losing a deposit is a strong incentive for lodgers to look after your room and behave properly.

- Holding a deposit will give you some protection if your lodger lets you down and you find yourself out of pocket.

As you may or may not be aware, there is a tenancy deposit protection scheme, which must be used by landlords who take a deposit from tenants in houses or flats. However, this only applies to ASTs. As you are letting to a lodger in your own home, this scheme will not apply to you.

However, it is important that you treat the deposit properly. Remember that it is not your money, but is the property of your lodger and should, if the room is returned to you in good condition when your lodger leaves, be paid back to him. This will be difficult if you have put the money into your own current account and spent it. For this reason, if you take a deposit, it should be kept entirely separate from your own money. The best way to do this is to open a special bank account, just for keeping deposits. Choose an interest bearing account if you can. The interest will belong to the lodger, unless your Lodger Agreement specifies that the landlord can keep it (which many do).

The fact that an applicant is on benefit or a low income is not necessarily a bar to taking a deposit. There are a number of organisations which will provide either the deposit money itself or a guarantee; for example, many local authorities have deposit guarantee schemes. You will be able to get a list of the organisations providing this service from your local Citizens Advice Bureau.

Housing benefit

If you receive benefit

If you are in receipt of housing benefit, you must inform the benefit office that you are renting out a room as this may affect the benefit you are entitled to. Note that if you do not do this, you will be committing benefit fraud, which is a criminal offence.

If your lodger receives benefit

There is quite a lot of demand for accommodation for people on benefit, in particular young people, people recently separated or divorced, or people who need support of some kind. It will therefore be fairly easy to find a lodger if you agree to accept lodgers on benefits.

However, the downside is that the benefit office will probably pay less than you would be able to get from a private paying lodger. Therefore, if you are thinking about taking a lodger on benefit, you might want to have a word with the benefit office first to see how much they will pay, before you make up your mind. If you can't get anywhere with the benefit office, your local Citizens Advice Bureau may be able to help. Benefit is now being paid under the new Local Housing Allowance (LHA) rules (which came into force in October 2007) where specific rates will be set for your area.

Note that if your lodger is to claim benefit/LHA, he will need to have a written agreement to show the benefit office. The benefit office will probably refuse to process his application until this has been received.

It is also worth mentioning here that the benefit office cannot change your agreement with your lodger. So, for example, if your lodger has agreed to pay you £60 per week, and you have only accepted him as a lodger on this basis, but the benefit office will only make a payment of £50 per week, this does not mean that he is no longer liable to you for the £60 per week. The legal situation is that there will be a shortfall which he will need to make up out of his own money. If he does not do this, he will be in arrears of rent, and this may be a reason for you to ask him to leave.

In reality, however, there is normally little point in asking a lodger to pay more than the benefit being paid to him.

Note that it is no longer possible, in the majority of cases, to have your lodger's benefit paid to you direct by the benefit office. This will only be done if there are more than eight weeks' rent outstanding or if the Council accepts that the lodger is 'vulnerable'. It is quite a long process getting someone assessed as vulnerable, and for more information speak to your benefits office.

You will find a useful online resource centre for housing benefit/LHA online at www.dwp.gov.uk/local-authority-staff/housing-benefit/claims-processing/local-housing-allowance.

Income Tax

One of the nice things about taking in a lodger is that you can take advantage of the government's 'Rent a Room' scheme. This allows you up to, currently, £4,250 income per year (£2,125 if letting jointly) from renting a room in your home, tax free.

The main downside is that you cannot claim both this and the Landlord's Energy Saving Allowance (under which landlords can claim back the costs of buying and installing energy-saving items) for the same period. While this will probably only affect larger landlords you can choose not to use the Rent a Room scheme in a year where there is Landlord's Energy Saving Allowance (or other expenditure) which would produce a net loss, as this can be carried forward.

Those who submit a tax return should indicate that they wish to use the Rent a Room scheme. However, most people renting out a room will just have any tax due deducted by their employer under the PAYE scheme.

If you are not using the Rent a Room scheme, or if your income from lodgers will exceed this sum, you will have to keep proper accounts. This means you should take extra care to keep all receipts for expenses related to your lodger (e.g. for decorating his room, invoices for gas safety checks, etc.) as they can be offset against your tax.

If the rent is higher than £4,250, you either elect to pay tax on the surplus above £4,250 (without relief for expenses) or you can treat the arrangement as being a furnished letting and prepare accounts.

This relief is available whether you rent out just one room to a lodger or you run a bed and breakfast business from your home.

For more information on the Rent a Room scheme see the Direct Gov website, Rent a Room scheme page at www.directgov.uk. If you require more detailed information you should speak to your accountant.

Council Tax

Taking in a lodger may affect the amount of Council Tax you pay if you receive a discount on your Council Tax bill; for example, if you live alone and have a discount, then if your lodger is living with you as his main home, you may no longer be entitled to this discount. If your lodger is a full-time student, he will be exempt from paying Council Tax. For more information you should speak to someone at the office dealing with Council Tax at your local authority.

CHAPTER 5

Finding and vetting your lodger

Finding lodgers

Friends and family

It is generally best to steer clear of taking in a friend or family member as a lodger. Renting a room to a lodger is a business transaction. You need the money. If for any reason your friend/family lodger fails to pay rent, or observe any house rules you may have (see chapter 6 for more information), it may be difficult for you to treat him in the same firm way that you would a stranger. Consider also whether you will be able to get him out at the proper time.

Unless you are very sure that problems will not arise, the best advice is not to let to someone who is a family member or a personal friend.

Local colleges and universities

These are a very good source of lodgers. Many students prefer to rent a room in someone's home rather than take on the responsibility of renting a flat or house with friends. There may also be staff and researchers looking for accommodation. You should contact the accommodation office and ask to be put on their list. There may also be a notice board where you can pin an advertisement. Note that most accommodation offices will want to inspect your property first to check that it is of a proper standard. You should ring them up and have a chat with them to see what their arrangements are.

Note that you may also be able to provide short-term accommodation to students on courses at local colleges and universities. For example, for several years I regularly took in Austrian teachers on a two-week language course at my local university. With this sort of arrangement you will need to liaise with the relevant course provider, who will allocate the students to you and will normally also be responsible for payment.

Hospitals

If you live near a hospital, this will also be a good source of lodgers. Doctors and nurses will often require accommodation, and relatives of patients may need short-term accommodation to be near patients. Ask to see if there is someone in charge of helping people find accommodation and see if you can go on his list. At the very least there should be a notice board where you can put a card.

Local large employers

If there is a large factory or government department or other large local employer nearby, it is worth talking to the personnel officer. It is likely that he will often be looking for lodgings for staff or visitors to the company. Again, he may have a database you can go on, or there may be a staff notice board where you can put a card.

The Local Housing Authority

They will often be looking for available accommodation where they can refer people, particularly people who have been made homeless. Bear in mind, however, that most of these people will be on housing benefit/LHA.

The internet

The internet is becoming increasingly important for all types of rented accommodation, not least rooms for lodgers. The following are a list of some popular sites:

- www.mondaytofriday.com

- www.spareroom.co.uk

- www.roombuddies.com

- www.rooms-to-let.com

- www.gumtree.com

You will find others by doing a search on the internet.

Newspapers and magazines

Some newspapers and magazines will have 'accommodation wanted' sections. Alternatively, you could put an advertisement yourself in a local paper, or local free magazine. Or if you are looking for a particular type of lodger, there may be a suitable magazine you can advertise in.

Local shops

A postcard in the window of a local post office or sweet shop is a traditional way of finding a local lodger. Supermarkets will also often have a place for cards.

What services will you provide?

This is perhaps a good place to reflect on what services you will be providing your lodgers, as you will generally want to mention this in your ad. As mentioned elsewhere, it is a good idea to provide some services as this will give you an excuse to visit the room from time to time. Here are some of the services you could offer:

- **Clean sheets and (perhaps) towels** – I would recommend that you always provide these. Most lodgers will not want to buy their own, and will appreciate your dealing with this. It will also give you a valid reason for visiting the room from time to time. You can make the bed as well, but I suggest that you leave this to them, and just leave the clean sheets in their room once a week or fortnight, and arrange for them to leave the dirty sheets outside or in your laundry basket.

- **Other washing** – some lodgers will appreciate your doing this for them, and you may prefer this to allowing them to use the washing machine themselves (the other option!).

- **Room cleaning** – this is another service which will give you a good reason to keep an eye on the room. However, many lodgers will prefer to keep their own room tidy, particularly as you would no doubt be charging for cleaning. If your lodger would like cleaning and this is not something you want to do personally, you can always employ a professional cleaner, provided your lodger's rent covers the cost of this.

- **Breakfast** – this is often a good idea: you can charge extra for it, and lodgers will appreciate it. If you are taking in students on a course, the course organisers will often require you to provide this. The breakfast does not have to be cooked; indeed generally people will not want this. Most people will be happy with fruit juice, tea/coffee, cereal (variety packs which have a selection of different types in small boxes are a good idea until you get to know what your lodger likes) and toast. Other ideas are a selection of individual yoghurts and tinned fruit (such as grapefruit). When I had students I used to lay the table before I went to bed at night, and the students would help themselves, making their own tea or coffee and toast, if I was not around.

- **Other meals** – providing breakfast is fairly straightforward, but you need to think carefully before making a commitment to providing other meals. If you do not like cooking, I would not advise it. If you enjoy cooking, it may be an opportunity to experiment and try out different dishes! If you are cooking for your family anyway, it will normally be no trouble. When I took in students on courses, this often included meals, and talking to the students (who were generally here to learn English) over dinner was an important part of their experience of staying in an English home. However, these courses were generally only a few weeks and were never more than two months. I loved cooking for them when they were there, but was generally pleased to stop doing it when they left!

Your advertisement

This should contain the following:

- The approximate location of your property (never give your full address).

- The rent; say 'exc. bills' if this does not include bills and 'inc. bills' if it does.

- Any special features such as an en suite bathroom, private parking, quiet location, near shops, etc. If you are paying for advertising, these can be abbreviated to save space (e.g. 'pte pkg', 'nr shops', etc.).

- Contact information – this will normally be a telephone number, but could be a box number, fax and/or email address.

> **Note:** it may be a good idea to use a Hotmail, Google or Yahoo email address (these can all be created free of charge) if your normal email address says too much about you. At this stage you do not want potential lodgers (or more particularly, criminals) to be able to find out who you are.

If you are booking an advertisement in a local paper:

- There will often be a special day for property adverts – find out when this is.

- Don't let the sales staff sell you unnecessary adverts – remember they are working on commission.

- Make sure that all spellings and numbers, particularly your telephone number, are correct.

If your advert is a card in a shop window or notice board, make sure it is clear and legible. Printed typescript is better than handwriting.

Choosing, checking and vetting lodgers

It is particularly important that you check your prospective lodger very carefully. This person is going to be living in your home and will have access to all your personal possessions when you are not there. He will have the key to your home. You need to be very careful to ensure that this person is totally trustworthy. You should also bear in mind that con men succeed because they are personable and plausible.

The telephone call

The initial contact will normally be by telephone. At this stage bear in mind that many criminals answer this sort of advertisement as preparation for burglaries, so be careful about what you say and whom you agree to meet. It is better to be safe than sorry. A few points on personal safety:

- Take a telephone number from the caller and then dial 1471 afterwards. Be a bit wary if the number is not the same.

- Do not give any personal information over the phone and in particular do not say that you live alone.

- If the caller is obscene, just put the phone down and dial 1471. If this reveals his telephone number, consider telling the police and your telephone company. If he starts to ring persistently, tell them anyway.

- If there is anything about the caller's voice that you do not like, just say that the room is no longer available.

During this initial telephone call you need to find out as much as possible about the applicant to see if he will be suitable. Here is a list of the sort of things you should cover:

- His name.

- His address.

- The contact details (including telephone and email address).

- Is he working, on benefit, or a student?

- Can he pay a deposit?

- Why does he need accommodation?

- Can he give you references?

You may want to add other things such as whether he is a smoker or non-smoker. It is best to have a list prepared so you can write the answers down while you are on the phone.

If you like the sound of him, you may want to make arrangements for him to visit the property there and then. Otherwise, make sure you have his telephone number and say you will ring him back.

The interview

Remember that your lodger applicant will be checking on you as well, and may have several places to visit. So make sure your house or flat is clean and tidy and as welcoming as possible.

You will often make your mind up fairly quickly when interviewing prospective lodgers. However, even if you like them and feel sure that you will accept them, you should take full details and deal with the interview in a professional way.

Note: it is often a good idea to have someone you trust with you at the interview, particularly if you live alone.

You should have the details you took over the telephone with you, and a pen and paper so you can write down other information. If you often interview lodgers, you may want to have a standard form which you can photocopy and use, or you can ask the applicant to complete a formal Lodger Application Form (see opposite).

If you are going to use a tenant-checking organisation (these are discussed below), you will need to obtain the applicant's consent first, so a formal application form will probably be a good idea as this consent can be incorporated.

Lodger Application Form

LODGER'S FULL NAME:

DATE OF BIRTH: | PLACE OF BIRTH:

CURRENT ADDRESS:

DURATION AT CURRENT ADDRESS:

TEL: | MOBILE:

EMAIL:

NAME OF CURRENT LANDLORD:

ADDRESS:

TEL: | MOBILE:

EMAIL:

NAME OF PREVIOUS LANDLORD:

ADDRESS:

TEL: | MOBILE:

EMAIL:

NEXT OF KIN (OR PERSON TO BE CONTACTED IN EMERGENCY):

NAME:

ADDRESS:

RELATIONSHIP:

TEL: | MOBILE:

EMAIL:

CURRENT EMPLOYER:

EMPLOYER'S ADDRESS:

EMPLOYER'S TEL:

EMPLOYER'S EMAIL:

JOB TITLE:

continued on next page

LENGTH OF TIME WITH CURRENT EMPLOYER:
NAME OF WORK SUPERVISOR:
WORK TEL:
HOUSING BENEFIT STATUS:
LOCAL AUTHORITY:
CRIMINAL CONVICTIONS:
BANK NAME:
BANK ADDRESS:
BANK ACCOUNT NUMBER:
BANK ACCOUNT STATUS:
EVIDENCE OF INCOME:
EVIDENCE OF IDENTITY OFFERED
PASSPORT NUMBER:
NATIONAL INSURANCE NUMBER:
CAR MAKE AND REGISTRATION:
OTHER:

I consent to your obtaining and retaining information about me.

I consent to your carrying out credit and reference checks on me, in confidence.

I believe that the facts stated above are true.

SIGNED:
DATE:

Here is a list of suggested points to cover at the interview. There may be others that you will want to add.

- You need to be sure that the prospective lodger will be able to pay the rent, so you should not feel embarrassed about asking him for financial details such as his salary.

- You should also ask to see some identification such as a passport, or driving licence.

- Discuss standards of cleanliness and whether you will expect him to share the cleaning or whether you will do this (the cost to be reflected in the rent).

- Whether you will or will not allow pets.

- Your policy on visitors, particularly overnight visitors. Find out if he is likely to have overnight visitors – if he will be regularly having his girlfriend stay overnight, do you want this?

- Arrangements for the use of the kitchen, if you are not providing meals.

- Whether he can use your landline telephone or not (although most people now have mobiles).

- Bills – whether these are included or paid separately. If paid separately, you need to be clear about how this is to be dealt with.

- His own electrical equipment. You won't want their using power-hungry appliances which will run up your bills; neither will you want them to use unsafe equipment which could cause a fire. If in doubt, insist on an electrical safety test.

- Computers and broadband. Many people will want internet access, and offering this will make your accommodation more attractive. However, if you do not have broadband or do not want to share access with your lodger, there are mobile services available, so do not feel you have to provide this.

- Tell them what, if any, services will be provided by you (see the separate section on this above).

- If the applicant gets upset about the question on your form about previous convictions, tell them it is a requirement imposed on you by your insurers.

Deposits – as discussed in chapter 4 above, it is generally a good idea to take a deposit, and you should make this clear at the meeting. If the lodger genuinely cannot afford this, there are a number of schemes to help, particularly for lodgers on benefit. Have a list of these ready to give to people (your local Citizens Advice Bureau will be able to let you know what schemes are operating in your area). Note that as you are letting to a lodger and not to a tenant on an AST, the tenancy deposit protection rules will not apply and you do not have to protect the deposit with one of the government-authorised schemes.

At the end of the interview – you should never accept anyone on the spot, even if you are pretty sure you will offer him the room. Always take his number and say you will ring him back. Make sure you do this, even if you are ringing to say that you have let to someone else.

Making a decision

After you have interviewed several people you will need to decide whom you will give the room to. This is a very important decision as this person will be sharing your home. Here are some things to consider:

- Having a lodger is a business relationship, so don't choose a lodger in the same way that you would choose a friend.

- Do you feel that you would be able to insist on payment of rent if he falls behind and to ask him to leave if he behaves badly? If you feel intimidated by him, it might be best to choose someone else.

- Does he have any mannerisms which might grate on you after a while?

- What is his lifestyle like? Is it one which is compatible with yours?

- Do you feel happy about his having the run of your house when you are not there?

- Do you feel uneasy about him?

It is perhaps the last point which is the most important. If you are uneasy about him, this is probably your subconscious warning you. Remember that it is very easy to let someone in but can be difficult to get him out again. It is better to accept no one than have a bad experience with a lodger and perhaps end up out of pocket.

Discrimination – you should never reject someone on the basis of race, nationality, colour or religion. In particular, your advertisements should not be discriminatory. Although the discrimination legislation does not apply to landlords letting rooms in their own home, your reasons for rejecting an applicant should be based on whether you think he can pay the rent and whether or not you like him, rather than the colour of his skin.

Once you have made your choice, ring up the person you have selected and offer him the room. Make it clear that the offer is subject to satisfactory references.

Remember, however, that the applicants will be looking at other rooms and your preferred applicant may have found somewhere else, so do not ring up your second choices and tell them the room has gone until you are sure that your first choice is definitely taking the room.

When telling applicants that the room has been let to someone else, try to be tactful and pleasant – remember that you want them to speak well of you when discussing you with other people, for example the student accommodation office, if you let to students.

References

Always follow up references. You cannot be too careful about checking out the person who will be living in your home.

The main things that you will be concerned about when taking in lodgers is whether they will pay the rent and whether they will look after your property properly. Nothing can absolutely guarantee this; however, taking and checking references will help to reduce the risk. There are three main types:

1. **Financial** – such as an employer or bank.

2. **Personal** – from a responsible person who has known the applicant for at least three years.

3. **A previous landlord** – find out why he left.

You need to be quite hard-hearted when checking references and assume, for the purpose of checking, that they are all false. In particular, do not trust a letter of recommendation handed to you. This could have been written by a friend or even by the applicant himself!

Double-check the contact details if you can; for example, look up employer's details in the Yellow Pages or on the internet. Make sure that you are speaking to the real employer, not just a friend of the prospective lodger.

Ring up and speak to the people given as references. They may tell you things that they would not want to put in writing. Be aware, though, that they may not be telling you everything; for example, a current landlord may be desperate for the prospective lodger to leave! Listen to their tone of voice and whether they are careful in their use of words when answering your questions.

Of the financial references, the employer will be the most important. You need to be sure that he can afford your rent. Bank references tend to be very bland and uninformative, but are worth taking if only to be sure that the applicant actually has a bank account.

It is also a good idea to use a credit reference agency. You will find these on the internet, for example the Check my Tenant service from Experian (www.checkmytenant.co.uk), or the Tenant Verify service provided by the LandlordZone website (www.tenantverify.co.uk). These will let you know if there are any County Court Judgments (CCJs) outstanding, check his creditworthiness and validate his identity, plus the Tenant Verify service has a delinquent tenant database.

Employer's reference

[Your address]

To: [Employer's name and address]

Date:

Dear Sirs

[Head the letter with the name of the prospective lodger]

The above has applied to rent a room in my house as a lodger and has given your details as his current employer.

I should be very grateful if you could support his application by providing the following information:

1. The start date of his employment.

2. His position in your company.

3. His salary.

4. Is his position temporary or permanent?

5. Is he in a probationary period?

6. If he is in a probationary period, when will this end?

I look forward to hearing from you as soon as possible. I enclose a stamped addressed envelope for your use.

Yours faithfully

[Your name and signature]

Bank reference

[Your address]

To: [Bank name and address]

Date:

Dear Sirs

[Head the letter with the name of the prospective lodger]

The above has applied to rent a room in my house as a lodger and has given your details to provide a financial reference. I enclose a copy of his signed authorisation.

Please can you make the necessary enquiries with your client's account. Any information provided will be treated in the strictest confidence.

I look forward to hearing from you as soon as possible. I enclose a stamped addressed envelope for your use.

Yours faithfully

[Your name and signature]

Lodger's authorisation to bank

I_____.

Hereby authorise _____Bank PLC

To provide a financial reference in respect of my application to rent a room from

[Enter your name and address here]

I understand that there may be a charge for this service and I authorise you to deduct this from my account accordingly.

Signed:_____

Dated:_____

Former landlord

[Your address]

To: [Former landlord's name and address]

Date:

Dear [Name]

[Head the letter with the name of the prospective lodger]

The above has applied to rent a room in my house as a lodger and has given your details as his former landlord.

I should be very grateful if you could support his application by providing the following information:

1. The length of time that he was with you.

2. The amount of rent.

3. Was his rent always paid on time?

4. Were there any problems? If so, please give details.

5. If you took a deposit, were there any deductions?

6. Would you let to him again?

I look forward to hearing from you as soon as possible. I enclose a stamped addressed envelope for your use.

Yours sincerely

[Your name and signature]

Personal reference

[Your address]

To: [Name and address]

Date:

Dear [Enter name]

[Head the letter with the name of the prospective lodger]

The above has applied to rent a room in my house as a lodger and has given your details to provide a personal character reference.

I should be very grateful if you could support his application by providing the following information:

1. Your relationship to the applicant.

2. How long have you known the applicant?

3. Do you consider the applicant to be trustworthy?

4. Is there any reason why I should not accept him as a lodger in my house?

I look forward to hearing from you as soon as possible. I enclose a stamped addressed envelope for your use.

Yours sincerely

[Your name and signature]

CHAPTER 6
Lodger Agreements

Should you have a formal agreement?

Taking in a lodger is far less formal than renting out a property to a tenant. Many lodgers never sign any form of agreement and the arrangement works perfectly well. I have to say that when I took in student lodgers, I did not get them to sign anything; they just paid me cash on a Saturday! Also if you are taking in students on a course, you will often be paid by the college or university running the course, and will not therefore have a direct agreement with the student staying with you.

However, in most cases, although it is not absolutely necessary, there is no doubt that having a written agreement is a very good idea. If relations break down between you and your lodger, it can be important to have an agreed document to refer to which sets out your respective rights and obligations. Bear in mind that unlike tenancies, there are hardly any 'implied terms' in Lodger Agreements; there is only what you have actually agreed between you. And if this is not written down, it can be difficult to prove exactly what that was.

Note: 'implied term' is the phrase used when terms are included in a contract even though they are not written down and/or included in any written contract document. In particular, Acts of Parliament often provide that certain terms will be implied into all contracts of a certain type; for example, Section 11 of the Landlord and Tenant Act 1985 implies repairing obligations into tenancy agreements.

Using an agreement

If you decide that you would like to have a Lodger Agreement, you can either buy a commercially produced one, or write your own.

Many people prefer to buy an agreement such as the Lawpack *Lodger Agreement*, available at www.lawpack.co.uk (I also provide one with my www.lodgerlandlord.co.uk service), as they prefer to have something which has been professionally drafted, and which they can feel confident complies with all the relevant legislation. If you decide to prepare your own, this is fine, but make sure it includes all the relevant clauses. For more information see the list further down.

Unfair terms

Some of you may be aware of the Unfair Terms in Consumer Contracts Regulations 1999. These regulations, which are enforced by the Office of Fair Trading, say that all standard clauses in agreements made between a business and a consumer must be 'fair' or they will not be binding on the consumer. Most Lodger Agreements will fall outside the scope of these regulations – if you are just letting out a room in your house or flat, this will not be considered to be a business.

However, if you rent out rooms to several lodgers, particularly if this is your main income (and can therefore be considered to be a business), you could well be bound by the regulations. In this case you need to take care that your agreement is compliant. For this reason I set out below some brief guidance on the regulations and how they work.

Core terms

The regulations do not apply to terms that form the main

subject matter of the agreement. So in a lodger context, this will be the names of the parties, the address of the property, and the amount of rent and damage deposit (if any) payable.

The test of fairness

This applies to all terms that are not core terms. Basically the landlord must not take advantage of the fact that he is presenting the lodger with a set of pre-drafted clauses (which many will sign without reading properly) by including clauses that take away any rights the lodger might otherwise have had. Note also that when assessing fairness, clauses are interpreted widely. If there is a possible unfair interpretation, then the clause will be considered unfair even if the landlord may not have intended this and may not be using the clause in this way. This is often where people inexperienced in drafting go wrong: they fail to realise that the clause they have written has more than one interpretation.

Individually negotiated clauses

The regulations will not apply to these – it is only standard clauses that are at risk.

Transparency

The regulations also provide that the agreement must be understandable. This means that it must be written in clear language, and not use legal or other jargon that the ordinary person would find difficult to understand. It is also arguable that if the agreement is difficult to read (e.g. if it is printed in small text in a pale colour) this will also be unfair. Also any clauses which are unusual, particularly if they impose an unusual financial obligation on the consumer, must be made clear and not buried in the ordinary clauses of a long agreement where they will not be noticed.

Prohibitions and permissions

One important drafting point worth mentioning here is in relation to prohibitions in tenancy or Lodger Agreements. If you are prohibiting something (such as keeping pets), it is very important that the clause includes the words along the lines of, 'save with the written permission of the landlord, which will not be withheld unreasonably'.

Now in the case of pets, for example, many landlords will say that they do not want this wording in the agreement as they know that they will never want their lodger to keep a pet. However, the effect of this will be that the clause will be unfair and invalid (and the tenant/lodger will be able to keep a pet if he wants). We know this because of a Spanish case (which applies to all EU countries, as these regulations came from an EU Directive). This case said that an outright prohibition against pets would be unfair because it would prevent a tenant's keeping a goldfish in a bowl.

Therefore, in any clause including a prohibition, unless it is something the tenant should not do anyway (such as keep illegal drugs), it is important that the wording providing for the tenant/lodger to request the landlord's permission and the statement that permission will not be withheld unreasonably is included. It does not mean that the landlord has to grant permission if asked. If you don't want a tenant to do something, this will normally be for a reasonable reason anyway (e.g. that you are allergic to cats, or just don't like them – it is, after all, your home). So long as your reason for refusing consent is justifiable, that is fine.

In conclusion, you must remember that these regulations only apply if you are letting out rooms as a business. This will normally be the case if you have several lodgers and the income from lodgers forms all, or the main part, of your income (for more guidance speak to your accountant). If you only have one or two lodgers to help you pay your rent or mortgage, you do not need to worry about them.

Essentials in a Lodger Agreement

This is a non-exclusive list of things that will need to be agreed between you and your lodger, and set out in your agreement (if you have one).

Particulars

Parties

You must know the full name of your lodger. If you use an agreement, your name and the name of the lodger must be clearly set out and spelled correctly. Put full names, and include Mr, Ms, Mrs, Dr, etc. as appropriate.

The property

Your address should be clearly set out in any agreement. You can specify the room if you wish, or just say the room agreed that the lodger will occupy.

If there are any parts of the property where you do not want the lodger to go, this must be made clear from the start. It may be a good idea to specifically set out in your agreement the parts of the property he will share with you and any other occupiers. Any other rooms in the property will be private.

The rent

You need to be very clear about the amount, whether it is to be paid weekly or monthly, and how it is to be paid, for example by cash, standing order, cheque.

The deposit

If taken, this is generally in the region of one month's rent. Note that as this is not an AST, the deposit is not covered by the tenancy deposit regulations and does not therefore need to be protected in one of the tenancy deposit schemes. See further on the deposit in chapter 4.

Any services

If you are going to provide any services such as clean sheets, towels or cleaning, this should be set out in the Lodger Agreement. If you provide meals, you need to be clear about whether these are included in the rent or not. Note that if the lodger is not going to share any living space with you, it is particularly important that you use an agreement and make it very clear that these services are provided. Otherwise he may acquire a tenancy with additional rights that you will not want him to have.

The period

Sometimes a Lodger Agreement will be for a specific period of time; sometimes it will just run from week to week or month to month until either party decides to end it. However, you will probably want your lodger to commit to a minimum period (otherwise you could spend your life advertising for and vetting prospective lodgers).

If your agreement gives a longish period such as six months or more, it is a good idea to have some sort of get-out clause, allowing either party to end the agreement early, say on 28 days' notice. Then if you find that you do not get on, the agreement will be easy to end.

The inventory

This is discussed in more detail below.

These are the main things which generally appear in the 'particulars' section of a professionally drafted agreement. Below are some other important points that you need to agree on:

Things to be agreed

House rules

Printed Lodger Agreements do not normally go into a lot of detail about domestic arrangements, as every situation will be different. However, they will be very important in your day-to-day life. It is a good idea to draw up a list of 'house rules' which can be agreed with your lodger and then included with the Lodger Agreement. If you do this, write something like 'see also house rules attached to this agreement' on your Lodger Agreement, and make sure that the house rules are also signed and dated by your lodger at the same time as the Lodger Agreement.

Remember that if you are letting out rooms as a business, the unfair terms regulations will apply to your house rules as well as to the main Lodger Agreement.

Bills

Some landlords include bills (such as electricity, gas, Council Tax) in the rent. Others, particularly where the lodger is staying a long time, will want the lodger to share these with them. In this case you will need to make it clear how the bills will be apportioned and get your lodger's agreement to this. Note that the details of this do not generally appear in a professionally drafted agreement; they will usually just have a paragraph stating that the lodger will contribute to these expenses, which you cross out if the rent is all-inclusive. You can put extra information about how you will work out what your lodger will actually pay in your house rules.

Insurance

You may be able to get the lodger's possessions covered under your insurance (speak to your insurers about this). If not, you must make it clear to your lodger that he is responsible for insuring his own possessions.

Note that it is sometimes a good idea to provide the lodger with a copy of your insurance policy (or an extract of the relevant parts) so if he does something that affects your insurance or causes the premium to increase, you will be able to hold him responsible for this. However, this is only really relevant for 'professional' landlords, where the unfair terms regulations will apply. This is because the Office of Fair Trading, in its published guidance on unfair terms in tenancy (and by implication lodger) agreements, stated that a party to an agreement cannot be bound by rules, such as in an insurance policy, which he has not seen.

Visitors

Most purchased agreements will prohibit visitors staying in the property without your permission. You should have already discussed this with your lodger, and have an idea of whether he is going to regularly have a partner stay over or not. If you agree to allow this, you may perhaps want to limit the number of nights per week that he stays over. This can go in your house rules.

Pets

Most purchased agreements will prohibit pets apart from with your written permission, which cannot be refused unreasonably.

However, this applies only to landlords taking in lodgers as a business; see the section above on unfair terms to see why. Note that if you have agreed specifically with your lodger that he may keep, say, a West Highland Terrier called Jack, and put this in the agreement, the unfair terms regulations will not apply to this clause any more, even if you are running a business. This is because this clause has been specifically discussed and agreed with your lodger; it is no longer just a standard clause. Any specific arrangements, such as where the dog is allowed to go in the house, can go in your house rules.

Use of the shared parts

This can include things such as agreed times for using the kitchen (if you don't provide meals), use of the bathroom and shared cleaning duties (if you do not provide cleaning). These should go in your house rules.

Use of telephone

This is less important now than in the past, as most people will have their own mobile phone. However, if your lodger wants to use your landline phone, you need to agree how this will be paid for (this can be set out in your house rules). Long-term lodgers may want to have a landline phone installed in their room, which you may or may not agree to.

Television

If your lodger wants to have a TV in his room, this is a reasonable request that you will normally agree to. However, if you do not have a TV yourself and therefore do not have a licence, this could get you into trouble! In this situation you will need to discuss it with your lodger, who will be responsible for the cost of it. Otherwise all TVs in the property will be covered by your licence.

Smoking

Whether or not you permit smoking will probably be governed by whether or not you smoke yourself. However, if you take in a smoker it will be difficult to prohibit him from smoking in his own room, although people are now becoming more accustomed to smoking prohibitions. What you can do is say that if he does smoke in his room (or allow visitors to smoke), you will be deducting the cost of professional cleaning of all the curtains and soft furnishings from the deposit when he leaves.

If you think that your lodger either will smoke or will have visitors who will smoke, it is a good idea, if you have a garden, to provide a table and chairs outside, where they can smoke if they wish. You should also have smoke alarms installed and check them regularly (although really, you should do this anyway).

Note that under the Smoking Regulations, areas which are used in common with other properties, such as stairways and halls in blocks of flats, must be smoke free and you should ensure that your lodger abides by this.

Business use

All professionally drafted tenancy agreements will prohibit this, largely because a residential tenancy can change into a business tenancy if business use is allowed, which is inadvisable. As this is not a tenancy, this is less likely to happen; however, I would still advise that any business use of your room is prohibited.

If your lodger sells the occasional Star Trek figure on eBay as a hobby, this is fine. But if he starts keeping large stocks of figures in his room, there are constant deliveries by post or carrier, and people start visiting to collect their order, you should suggest that he rents his own business premises, rather than use your home.

One very good reason why business use should be prohibited is that if he gets into financial difficulties, you will not want County Court Judgments registered against your home address, as this could affect your own credit rating.

Other legal clauses

There are a number of other clauses which generally appear in professionally drafted Lodger Agreements.

Licence statement

A professionally drafted Lodger Agreement should state that the agreement is a licence and not a tenancy, and say why (i.e. that the landlord shares living accommodation and/or provides services).

It is also a good idea to say that the licence is personal to the lodger signing the agreement and cannot be assigned to someone else, and also that it will end automatically if the lodger stops living at the property or if two or more months' rent are due and unpaid.

Costs and expenses

Most agreements will include a clause saying that interest should be paid on unpaid rent, for example 1% above bank base rate.

There is also often a general clause saying that the lodger will be responsible for the landlord's reasonable costs incurred as a result of the lodger not complying with the terms of the agreement. This clause, if properly drafted, will cover most things, as most bad behaviour which results in some sort of financial loss to the landlord will be in breach of one or more clauses in the Lodger Agreement.

Generally it is best not to include any other penalty clauses, particularly if you are taking in lodgers as a business, as this type of clause can easily fall foul of the unfair contract terms regulations if not carefully drafted.

Using the room and the property

Most professional agreements will also have a number of clauses dealing with behaviour in the property; for example, clauses stating that they should keep the room neat and tidy; prohibitions against any alterations or redecoration; prohibitions against doing anything that will cause a nuisance to other occupiers or neighbours; and doing anything illegal.

It is also a good idea to specifically prohibit keeping any dangerous or flammable items in the room (other than household objects such as matches), and also to specifically state that they should not use any heating appliances other than those provided, assuming of course that there are suitable heating appliances provided in the room.

Ending the agreement

As mentioned above, it is a good idea to include a procedure for ending the agreement; this is generally 28 days' written notice by either party. You should also include the statement, referred to above, saying that the lodger's licence will end automatically if more than two months' rent is due and unpaid.

Professionally drafted agreements often include a clause saying that the agreement will come to an end if the property is destroyed or becomes uninhabitable (although this should perhaps be obvious!).

Other clauses generally included provide for the lodger to leave the room clean and tidy when he goes, remove all his personal belongings and rubbish, and provide a forwarding address and contact telephone number.

Signing the agreement

You should have two copies of the agreement, one for you and one for the lodger (together with two copies of any separate house rules, which should be attached to the main agreement). You should both sign one and then exchange them so that you end up with the copy signed by the lodger and he ends up with the copy signed by you. Or you can both sign both copies. It is not normally necessary to get the signatures witnessed but there is no harm if you do.

Inventories

Inventories are becoming far more common nowadays than they used to be, certainly for rented properties where they are more or less essential if a landlord is to have any chance of success in disputed deductions from deposit claims at arbitration.

The situation is slightly different with lodgers. As they will be living in your home and under your eye, you may feel that a formal inventory is superfluous. However, remember that memories fade over time, and an inventory is the best way to decide whether there was a blue lampshade in the lodger's room when he went in or whether the desk had a deep scratch on the bottom right drawer or not.

There is no point in doing an inventory unless you make it as detailed as possible. Include all items in the lodger's room and state their condition and, if possible, the manufacturer (e.g. 'Sony bedside radio alarm clock'). You should also include the condition of the doors, windows, light fittings, curtains and carpet.

You could also take some photographs showing the condition of the room and its contents (some professional inventory clerks even do videos of the property), particularly if any of the furniture is valuable. Any photographs should be very clear and, if showing scratches or marks on furniture, include something to show the scale.

You should check the inventory over with the lodger before he moves in, and both of you should sign and date it. Keep your copy with your signed copy of the Lodger Agreement, together with any agreed photographs, which should be initialled and dated on the back by you both if used.

You can create your own inventory form, or you can buy one such as the Lawpack inventory form.

Other documents

When you deal with the Lodger Agreement and inventory, there will also be a number of other documents that are best dealt with at the same time:

A standing order form

If your lodger is to be a long-term lodger paying monthly, it is a good idea to get him to sign a standing order form with his bank. Keep a copy before you send it off to the bank. This will mean that the rent is paid regularly into your account. There is a template form opposite.

Rent book

If your lodger pays weekly, you should give him a rent book. Lawpack publishes a very good one, which is available from www.lawpack.co.uk.

Standing order form template

To _____

_____

[Tenant's bank name & address]

Please pay_____

_____

[Landlord's bank name & address]

To the credit of_____

_____

[Landlord's account name & account number]

☐☐ ☐☐ ☐☐

[& sort code]

The sum of _____

[Amount in figures & words]

Commencing _____

[Date of first payment]

And thereafter every _____

[Due date & frequency, e.g. '13th monthly']

Until _____

[Date of last payment, you may write 'until further notice']

Quoting the reference _____

_____

[The address of the Property being let]

Account name to be debited _____

[Tenant's name]

Account number to be debited _____

[Tenant's account number]

Signed _____   Dated _____

_____   _____

_____   _____

[Tenant(s)]

A housing benefit letter of authority

If your lodger is on benefit or Local Housing Allowance (LHA), it is very important that you get him to sign a letter of authority, authorising the benefit office to speak to you about his benefit application. If you don't do this, the benefit office will refuse to tell you anything, under the Data Protection Act. You will find a form of letter you can use below.

As it is not unknown for local authorities to lose documents when sent to them, it might be an idea to get your lodger to sign two (or even three) letters, just in case.

Housing benefit letter of authority template

To:

The Housing Benefit Office

[Name and address of office]

Date:

Dear Sirs

Re: [Address of property]

I am renting a room as a lodger at the above property.

I hereby authorise and request you to provide to my landlord [name of landlord] at the above address any information he or she may request regarding my application for housing benefit/Local Housing Allowance (LHA), and any other information he or she may request regarding my housing benefit/LHA entitlement and payment of housing benefit/LHA to me after my application has been processed.

If it takes longer than eight weeks to process my application, please can the initial payments be made direct to my landlord.

Yours faithfully

Signed:_____   Date: _____

[Name of lodger]

The gas certificate

If your property has gas appliances, you should have obtained a gas safety certificate from your Gas Safe Register registered engineer as discussed in chapter 2 above. Now is the time to give a copy of this certificate to your lodger.

Deposits and Energy Performance Certificates – a quick reminder here that landlords taking in lodgers do not need to protect any deposit taken, so there is no need to serve any notice regarding the tenancy deposit protection scheme (as there would be for a tenancy of a house or flat), although your lodger will probably want a receipt. There is also no obligation on you to provide an Energy Performance Certificate, as again these are not required for landlords of lodgers.

Keeping records

As mentioned elsewhere, it is important that you keep records of all forms and paperwork in a safe place where you can find them easily. You should have a separate file for each of your lodgers, which should contain their application form, references, and their Lodger Agreement and inventory, as well as any other paperwork relating to their occupation.

CHAPTER 7
Living with lodgers

So, your carefully chosen lodger has signed his Lodger Agreement, agreed your inventory, and moved in. This chapter looks at some of the issues and questions which may arise, although problem lodgers are looked at in the next chapter.

Making friends with your lodger

The reason the lodger has come to live in your house is a commercial one. You need his rent. He needs somewhere to live. How should you behave towards him?

It is possible that your lodger is wholly trustworthy, and that over time you will develop a lifelong friendship. However, it is equally possible that he will turn out to be wholly unsatisfactory. Remember that at some stage you may have to take a stand about something – putting up the rent, for example, or asking him not to do something, or even asking him to leave. If you have been too friendly, it may make it difficult for you to do these things.

You should therefore hold back from being too open towards him, at least until he has been with you for a while and has proved himself. Even then, always keep in mind that he is your lodger and you are his landlord, and do not do anything that may make this commercial relationship more difficult. The best attitude is to be friendly but reserved, and to keep your personal life separate.

Rent payments

If your lodger pays rent in cash once a week, keeping a track of rent payments will not normally be a problem. You will know when he has not paid! However, if your lodger pays by standing order or direct payment into your bank account, you should make a habit of checking regularly to see that the payments have actually gone through.

If your lodger pays weekly, you will need to give him a rent book, for example the Lawpack rent book.

If your lodger is on benefit, you may have to wait a while before any payments get through. Unfortunately, under the Local Housing Allowance rules rent payments are no longer paid direct to the landlord except in exceptional circumstances, so you will have to trust your lodger to pay the money over to you when he receives it. However, as your lodger will have signed a housing benefit letter of authority (see chapter 6), you should make sure that this is provided to the benefit office. If possible, take it in to the benefit office personally and get a receipt so they cannot deny that they have got it. You will then be able to ring them up to find out what is going on if your lodger says he cannot pay rent because his benefit payment has not come through.

It is a good idea to keep a written record of all conversations and also to make a note of the name of the person you are speaking to.

Note that if your lodger is more than eight weeks in arrears of rent, you should write to the benefit office and inform them of this, as they should then arrange to pay the rent to you direct. This is set out in the Housing Benefit Regulations, so if the benefit office refuse to do this you should lodge an official complaint.

As mentioned in chapter 4, unlike the old-style housing benefit, the new Local Housing Allowance cannot be paid direct to the landlord. If your lodger would prefer this, perhaps because he is worried that the money could get swallowed up by his overdraft, note that some Credit Unions will set up special accounts for the purpose of receiving benefit and passing it on to the landlord. I have a special information page on my www.landlordlaw.co.uk service which lists Credit Unions I am aware of that provide this service. You can find Credit Unions near you via www.abcul.org.

Putting up the rent

After your lodger has been with you for a while, you may find it necessary to put up your rent. The main reason for this will normally be because your own bills have gone up.

Having someone else living in the house will inevitably result in some increase in your utility bills – there will, after all, be at least some extra heating and lighting in your spare room (assuming this was unoccupied before), and you should take this into account when setting your rent. However, if your utility bills have gone up dramatically as a result of the lodger's use, say, of electricity, then if your rent is an inclusive one, you will need to consider increasing the rent fairly quickly. There is not much point in having a lodger if he is costing you money. If your lodger is unhappy about the rent increase, show him the utility bills before and after he arrived to prove your point.

With a long-term lodger, you will need to increase the rent every year or so simply to keep up with the cost of living. Your lodger should appreciate this and indeed will probably expect his rent to go up in this way.

However, if in either case your lodger refuses to pay the higher rent, then (assuming the increase you have asked for is a reasonable one) you should consider asking him to leave so you can find a new lodger, either at a higher rent, or someone who will not run your utility bills up so much.

If you agree an increase of rent during the fixed term of your written Lodger Agreement, this will technically be an agreed variation of contract. It is a good idea to have a written note of the agreed new rent, and for you both to initial this. This can then be kept with the rest of your paperwork.

If your lodger is minded to be difficult about an informal request to increase the rent, the best course of action is to formally terminate the Lodger Agreement as provided in your written agreement (or if you have no written agreement, as discussed in chapter 8 below), and say that you will only be prepared to agree to a new Lodger Agreement at the higher rent.

Privacy issues and entering the lodger's room

When someone is renting a room from you, he will expect some privacy. However, it is your home, and you need to be sure, for example, that there are no repairs which need to be done in the lodger's room, and that it is being used appropriately. Also, as discussed in chapter 1, it is important that you retain the right to go in there from time to time, so as to prevent the possibility of a tenancy arising.

The best way to go about this is by providing some sort of service. If you provide cleaning, then this will never be a problem. However, if your lodger does his own cleaning, it is a good idea to provide some other service, the most common and obvious of which is providing clean sheets and towels. You can either actually make his bed, or you can just leave the clean sheets on the bed and have an arrangement where he leaves the dirty sheets outside later.

Ideally you should enter the room once a week, or at least once a fortnight, although you must not pry among his personal things or indeed touch anything belonging to him. You should check visually that the room is in good condition (e.g. that the electrical sockets are not being overloaded), and that generally the room is being used in a responsible and proper manner.

You will probably go in from time to time when he is not there, particularly if you are doing the cleaning. You should be quite open about this, and provided that you are not prying or being too intrusive your lodger should accept this. However, if your lodger asks you not to go into the room at all, you should make it clear that this is your home and you will need to check its condition from time to time. If he insists on complete privacy, particularly if he puts a lock on the door, you should consider asking him to leave.

Asking lodgers to leave (amicable situations)

Inevitably a day will come when either your lodger will leave, or you will want him to go. Your lodger may only ever have been staying for a limited period of time (e.g. if he is a student), or you may no longer need a lodger, perhaps because you are getting married, or moving house, or simply because you no longer need the money.

In the vast majority of cases this will be an amicable arrangement. You will normally agree between yourselves the date when your lodger will be leaving and there will be no need for any formal letters. If it is an amicable situation, then you can agree any notice period that you like; it doesn't have to be 28 days. You may feel that you would like to confirm the arrangement, in which case you could give your lodger a letter along the following lines.

(For situations where you are asking your lodger to leave because of problems, please see the next chapter.)

Lodger check-out letter

Dear X

I write to confirm our agreement that you will be leaving on [date]. Please can you leave your room clean and tidy and take all your possessions with you when you go.

[Add this if there is a deposit]

I will need to check the inventory over with you before you leave to check that there is no damage or any missing items before returning your deposit. Please speak to me to arrange a mutually convenient time for us to do this/We have provisionally agreed to do this on [date].

[It is nice to put a 'thank you' paragraph here – this is just a suggested wording – you will probably want to do your own]

Thank you for being such an excellent lodger – it has been very pleasant having you staying with us. I wish you all the best for the future.

[If you have a visitors' book]

Please do not forget to sign our visitors' book before you go, so we will have something to remember you by!

Yours sincerely

[Your name and signature]

CHAPTER 8
Problem lodgers

Hopefully your experience of lodgers will be – as mine was – a largely pleasant one, and you will not need to take any sort of legal or other action against them. However, sadly, this is not always the case. If you do experience problems, one or more of the following courses of action may be necessary.

> **Note:** the procedures set out in this chapter will only apply to landlords with lodgers living in their own home where at least some living space (e.g. kitchen, bathroom, sitting room) is shared with the lodger. If you do not share living space, in particular if your lodger's door has a lock on it and you never enter his room, the information in this chapter will not apply to you and you should take legal advice.

First action – talk to them

If there is something you are unhappy about, it is best to speak to your lodger about it. Perhaps he is not complying with your house rules, or perhaps he is starting to pay his rent late.

Having a discussion with him may resolve the problem.

Writing a letter or note

If your conversation has not brought about any change, you may want to put your concerns in writing. This may also be a good idea if he is not in often, and you are not able to speak to him. Or you may find it easier to put your complaint in writing, particularly if you feel that he does not take any notice of what you say. This first letter need not be very formal. It could just be a note left on his bed saying something like:

[Date]

Dear X

I have received a complaint from one of the neighbours about your music being played late at night. If you want to play music after 9pm can you please either keep it very quiet or use headphones. Thank you.

[Your name and signature]

Or

[Date]

Dear X

I am concerned that you have not been paying your full rent to me on a Saturday as agreed. I need your rent for my own expenses and your failure to pay on time is causing me problems. Please can you let me have the outstanding rent of £[insert amount] immediately, and arrange to pay promptly in future. Thank you.

[Your name and signature]

Writing a second letter

If your chat and first note to your lodger has not brought about any improvement, you might want to try another letter. Or perhaps your first note brought about an initial improvement that has not lasted. This letter should be a bit more formal and suggest that you will not be willing to put up with things forever.

Note that you do not have to do this, and if you have already decided that you want him to leave you can omit this step and go straight to the section below on giving notice to leave.

[Date]

Dear X

I asked you two weeks ago if you could please play your music quietly or on headphones after 9pm. However, you are continuing to play it loudly and I have had further complaints from my neighbour. I am afraid that if you cannot behave in a more considerate manner I will have to think about asking you to leave.

Yours sincerely

[Your name and signature]

Or

[Date]

Dear X

You have not paid me the outstanding rent as asked in my note last week and have not paid the full rent for this week. Can you please pay all outstanding rent to me by Saturday at the latest, and arrange to pay future rent promptly. If this is not done, I will have to consider asking you to leave.

Yours sincerely

[Your name and signature]

The threat of being asked to leave may bring your lodger to his senses and you may have no further trouble. However, if he takes no notice of your second letter then you should consider seriously whether you want to continue to have him as a lodger. This is, after all, your home. If your lodger is behaving badly or failing to pay you your rent, you should not be expected to put up with this.

Giving notice to leave

If you have not managed to resolve your difficulties with your lodger, you will probably be looking to ask him to leave. Landlords of lodgers are in a fortunate position because unlike landlords of rented property, you do not need to get a County Court order for possession. However, you do need to give the lodger a formal notice to vacate first.

Normally the notice period will be specified in your agreement to be not less than 28 days, and if you have no agreement, this is the proper notice period to give him in most cases. If, for example, you are asking your lodger to leave because of relatively minor matters such as personality clashes or his failure to clean the kitchen properly, you should give him the full 28 days so he cannot criticise you (and I would recommend you give 28 days in this type of situation even if your Lodger Agreement gives a shorter period).

However, for more serious problems such as aggressive behaviour or violence towards you or your family, or if you find he is using your property for something illegal such as using or dealing in prohibited drugs, it will normally be acceptable for you to give him a shorter notice period. Note also that if there is a 28-day or longer notice period in the Lodger Agreement, you are not bound by this if his behaviour is such that he can be considered to be in breach of the Lodger Agreement (which will be the case for the examples given above).

For cases of rent arrears, if you are using a printed agreement (e.g. a Lawpack agreement) this will normally state that the lodger's licence to occupy your property will end automatically if he is in arrears of rent of two months. However, you will still need to give your lodger a formal letter asking him to vacate.

Below are some suggested letters. As mentioned in the box at the start of this chapter, these will only be suitable for lodgers, where they share living accommodation with you. If this is not the case, you should take legal advice.

Feel free to adapt the wording if it is does not fit your situation exactly, and/or where there is an asterisk select the wording that applies. However, the main wording giving notice should not be changed.

Standard letter giving notice

This letter can be used in the majority of cases, suitably adapted.

Dear X

Further to my previous letters to you/our conversation on [date]* I am writing to give you formal notice to leave. In law/Under the terms of the agreement between us,* your occupation can be ended by either of us by giving not less than 28 days' notice [or put in any different time which may be in the agreement].

[If you like, you can put in a paragraph here giving your reasons. However, if you do, make them brief and to the point. This paragraph should be no more than a few lines]

I should be grateful if you could please vacate your room by 11am on [date]. Please note that your right to stay in the room will terminate at that time. Please confirm the day and time you will be leaving and ensure that your room is left in a clean and tidy condition when you go. Please can you be sure to take all personal possessions with you.

[Add this paragraph if there is a deposit]

Note that I will need to check the inventory over with you before you leave to check that there is no damage or any missing items before returning your deposit. Please speak to me to arrange a mutually convenient time for us to do this.

[Add this paragraph if you think the lodger will create difficulties about leaving]

As you know, you are a lodger in my home. As I am, and have been from the start of your stay, a resident landlord (this being my only home), sharing accommodation with you, I do not need a court order to evict you (Protection from Eviction Act 1977, Section 3A).

Yours sincerely

[Your name and signature]

Suggested alternative version 1 – breach of agreement

This form of letter can be used if your lodger has behaved badly and you feel that a more strongly worded letter is appropriate, particularly if you wish to give a shorter notice period.

Dear X

As your landlord I am writing to notify you that in view of [put here the reason why you wish to end the agreement, e.g. 'your unacceptable behaviour, in particular the incident on [giving brief details of the incident]'] I wish to terminate your licence agreement to live in my property.

[Add this if you are giving less than the 28 days or less than the agreed notice period in your agreement, due to exceptionally bad or violent behaviour]

Your behaviour is a serious breach of the terms of your Lodger Agreement and I therefore require you to vacate within the next 14 days/7 days*.

[Only add this if you think there is a real possibility of serious violence towards you, your family and visitors]

If there is any recurrence of [put here what the problem behaviour was], I reserve the right to terminate your right to stay here with immediate effect, and I will be reporting the incident to the police.

I will require you to move out of your room not later than 11am on [put here the date, amend the time if wished]. Please can you remove all personal property and return the keys to me. If you use your keys to enter my property after that date and time, it will be without my licence or consent.

Note that as you are a lodger sharing living accommodation with me, and as I have been, from the start of your stay, a resident landlord (this being my only home), I do not need a court order to evict you (Protection from Eviction Act 1977, Section 3A).

[Add this paragraph if there is a deposit]

Note that I will need to check the inventory over with you before you leave to check that there is no damage or any missing items before returning your deposit. Please speak to me to arrange a mutually convenient time for us to do this.

I am sorry to have to ask you to leave in this way but your behaviour leaves me no alternative.

Yours sincerely

[Your name and signature]

Suggested alternative version 2 – rent arrears of two months or more

Dear X

I am concerned to note that once again you have failed to pay me your rent, and this brings your arrears to £[insert amount]. This is wholly unacceptable, as I rely on the income from you as my lodger to pay many of my own expenses.

The terms of your licence agreement specifically state that your licence (i.e. right) to live here will end if there are arrears of rent of two months or more. As your arrears are now two months'/over two months'* worth, this clause comes into effect and I must ask you to leave.

I am prepared to allow you to stay until [give date] to find somewhere else to live. However, I will require your room back after 11am on that date. Please can you remove all personal property and return the keys to me. If you use your keys to enter my property after that date and time, it will be without my licence or consent.

[Add this paragraph if there is a deposit]

Note that I will need to check the inventory over with you before you leave to check that there is no damage or any missing items to be deducted from your deposit. Please speak to me to arrange a mutually convenient time for us to do this. Any balance from your deposit will then be offset against your rent arrears.

Note that as you are a lodger sharing living accommodation with me, and as I have been, from the start of your stay, a resident landlord (this being my only home), I do not need a court order to evict you (Protection from Eviction Act 1977, Section 3A).

I am sorry to have to ask you to leave in this way, but as my reason for taking lodgers is to receive rent, I cannot afford to allow you to remain any longer.

Yours sincerely

[Your name and signature]

If your lodger refuses to leave

Hopefully your lodger will leave as asked on or before the day given, in which case please see the following chapter. However, in a few cases (and this happens only very rarely) your lodger may refuse to move out. Before moving to forcible eviction, as described below, you could consider the following options:

- If your lodger is a student, you could complain to his university or college. If you advertised through the accommodation office, have a word with them as they may be able to assist.

- If your lodger came to you via a local employer, you could consider speaking to them about the problem.

- If the lodger has given any next of kin in his application form, consider contacting them to see if they can help.

However, if the problem continues, you may have no option but to proceed to evict your lodger forcibly.

Note: the only time I had to ask someone to leave, he was a student on a course at a local college. The student concerned was behaving unreasonably and I did not feel I could continue to allow him to stay. The college arranged for him to go elsewhere, but I did not get any more students from them. So think carefully before doing this!

Forcible eviction

Hopefully this will never be necessary. However, if you are unfortunate enough to have a lodger who refuses to leave, you can follow the procedure set out below. Note that apart from in cases of exceptionally bad behaviour, you would be unwise to use this procedure unless your lodger has been given formal written notice to leave and that this was given to him at least 28 days previously. In all cases, at least one letter giving notice to vacate must have been given to the lodger and the notice period must have expired.

1. On or shortly before the day the lodger is supposed to move out, ask him when he will be vacating. If he asks for just a day or two longer, consider allowing him to stay if there is a good reason for this (e.g. if he cannot move into his new accommodation immediately). However, if you feel that you are being taken advantage of and/or if you do not wish him to remain any longer (particularly if you have already given him a lot of leeway), proceed as follows.

2. On a day which must be at least one full day after the date when you asked the lodger to leave (and preferably a bit longer, so you can show that you have been reasonable), arrange for the locks on your property to be changed at a time when your lodger is likely to be out for some time. (It is best not to warn your lodger of this beforehand in case he decides to stay in the property so as to prevent your doing this.)

3. When your lodger returns, refuse to let him in. If you think that he is likely to cause trouble, you should arrange for the police to be present (it may be a good idea to arrange for this anyway). The police should attend if you tell them that you expect there to be a breach of the peace.

If the police are not there and your lodger starts causing trouble, do not open the door; ring the police and ask them to come out immediately. Under no circumstances let your lodger back into the property.

It is very important that you use no force or violence when evicting your lodger. If you do, this will put you in breach of the law and you will be vulnerable to being arrested and prosecuted by the police. This is why a passive eviction process of refusing to allow him back in is recommended. If your lodger attacks you, you can defend yourself, but it is best to avoid any situation where this can happen (i.e. don't open the door). This is why having a police presence is important, so if your lodger becomes violent, they can deal with it for you.

4. Your lodger will be entitled to have his possessions returned to him. The best way to do this is to pack them up (e.g. in black bags) and pass them out to him. Unless you trust him not to cause any problem, he should only be allowed back into your property (e.g. to pack) if there is police presence.

5. Under no circumstances should you or anyone in your house let the lodger in again. If he continues to cause problems, consider going to a solicitor and asking for an injunction (see explanation box below). However, it is most unlikely that this will be necessary. In most cases the lodger will accept the situation, particularly if the police have been involved.

Injunction: this is a court order which prohibits someone from doing something (e.g. visiting or trying to enter your property). If the injunction is breached, you can ask for the defendant to be arrested and imprisoned. Injunction proceedings are fairly complex and should only be done with the help of a solicitor. They are generally expensive. Note also that the court will not normally make an injunction order unless you can show that there is a real danger that someone will be physically injured. They are most commonly used in family proceedings to protect a wife/girlfriend from a violent partner.

Comments on your legal right to forcibly evict

The above procedure sounds harsh, and indeed it is. It should only ever be used as a last resort, against a lodger who has behaved badly towards you and who has either been given several warnings and requests to vacate but has totally ignored them, or who has behaved so appallingly that it is unreasonable for anyone to expect you to allow him to stay any longer.

If you are worried about forcible eviction, it will probably be wise for you to take legal advice first, but make sure it is from someone who knows and understands housing and letting law (preferably a solicitor). As most lawyers do not specialise in this area of law, I would suggest you show them this section of this book (including in particular the extract from the statute below) and ask them if, in their opinion, the advice given here applies to you.

If you decide to proceed without taking legal advice first, and are challenged about your right to evict a lodger in this way without a court order (either by the lodger himself or by any 'legal adviser' on his behalf), tell him that your legal authority is contained in Section 3A(2) of the Protection from Eviction Act 1977.

In the first part of this Act, it states that no residential occupier shall be evicted other than by 'due process of law', i.e. by obtaining a court order for possession. Section 3 of the Act then goes on to list various types of occupation where this rule does not apply – they are described in the Act as 'excluded tenancies and licences'; sub-sections (2) and (3) are the sections which provide for lodgers to be excluded. This means that you do not need to get a court order to evict your lodger. This differs from a residential tenancy where you always need a court order to evict your tenant.

As this is an important matter, I set out below in full the relevant extract from the Protection from Eviction Act 1977. The sections dealing with lodgers are (2) and (3) but I am including other relevant parts of this section also, so you can see exactly what it says:

3A. Excluded tenancies and licences

(1) Any reference in this Act to an excluded tenancy or an excluded licence is a reference to a tenancy or licence which is excluded

by virtue of any of the following provisions of this section.

(2)   *A tenancy or licence is excluded if:*

    (a)   *under its terms the occupier shares any accommodation with the landlord or licensor; and*

    (b)   *immediately before the tenancy or licence was granted and also at the time it comes to an end, the landlord or licensor occupied as his only or principal home premises of which the whole or part of the shared accommodation formed part.*

(3)   *A tenancy or licence is also excluded if:*

    (a)   *under its terms the occupier shares any accommodation with a member of the family of the landlord or licensor;*

    (b)   *immediately before the tenancy or licence was granted and also at the time it comes to an end, the member of the family of the landlord or licensor occupied as his only or principal home premises of which the whole or part of the shared accommodation formed part; and*

    (c)   *immediately before the tenancy or licence was granted and also at the time it comes to an end, the landlord or licensor occupied as his only or principal home premises in the same building as the shared accommodation and that building is not a purpose-built block of flats.*

(4)   *For the purposes of subsections (2) and (3) above, an occupier shares accommodation with another person if he has the use of it in common with that person (whether or not also in common with others) and any reference in those subsections to shared accommodation shall be construed accordingly, and if, in relation to any tenancy or licence, there is at any time more than one person who is the landlord or licensor, any reference in those subsections to the landlord or licensor shall be construed as a reference to any one of those persons.*

(5) *In subsections (2) to (4) above:*

(a) *'accommodation' includes neither an area used for storage nor a staircase, passage, corridor or other means of access;*

(b) *'occupier' means, in relation to a tenancy, the tenant and, in relation to a licence, the licensee; and*

[Subsection (c) then goes on to describe, with reference to other statutes, the term 'purpose-built block of flats' and the definition of family members]

If you want to read more of this Act (or indeed any other), you will find it online in the Statute Law Database at www.statutelaw.gov.uk.

CHAPTER 9

When your lodger leaves

It will often be a sad time when your lodger leaves. He may have been with you for a long time and perhaps have become almost part of the family. You should try to make his departure as pleasant as possible, if only because he will then be more likely to recommend you to his friends!

The following will probably need to be done.

If you have taken a deposit

You will need to check the condition of the room against the inventory first. In most cases your lodger will have left it in a spotless condition and you will be able to refund his deposit to him there and then. Otherwise proceed as follows:

- If you know what the value of the damage is (e.g. if it is a broken lamp which you know you can replace for £20), you can simply deduct this sum before paying him the deposit there and then.

- If you do not know the cost of replacing the item or doing the repair work, you should tell him that you cannot refund his deposit until this has been ascertained. Take contact details from him and say that you will get in touch with him as soon as you know. Make sure you do this promptly; if it takes longer than a week, ring him and let him know the reason for the delay.

- When you know the cost, send the balance to him at his

forwarding address or give it to him in cash if he prefers to call round for it.

- If there are arrears of rent, these should be deducted from the deposit after any loss or damage has been taken out.

Fair wear and tear

It is probably worth mentioning here the rule regarding fair wear and tear, in respect of deductions from deposits. This provides that when considering deductions, you should not expect a property (in the case of a tenancy) or a room (in your case) to be in the same pristine condition it was when the lodger moved in, particularly if he has been living there for some time.

If the lodger has been living in the room for two years, you can only expect a room to be given up in the condition you would expect it to be after someone has lived in it for two years. If the room was newly decorated before he moved in, you cannot, for example, insist that he pay for the room to be redecorated again after he has gone. This is an expense which you as landlord must bear.

Therefore deductions will only be for items which have been broken other than by the lodger using the room in a reasonable manner. So if a bedside rug needs replacing because it is worn and a bit tattered, this will normally be fair wear and tear. However, if it has been stained by the lodger dropping a full bottle of indelible ink on it (which cannot be removed by cleaning), then he will be responsible for the (reasonable) cost of a new rug, assuming that the rug was not so worn out that it was due to be replaced anyway.

So far as cleaning and redecoration is concerned, provided the room is left in a reasonable condition, you will only really be entitled to charge for this if your lodger has been smoking in the room against your wishes, and the décor and furnishings have been damaged by the smoke.

Visitors' book

If you regularly have lodgers or paying guests, it is nice to keep a visitors' book and get them to write in it before they go. It is amazing how you forget people as time goes by and you will enjoy looking over your book in years to come, remembering all the people who have stayed with you.

Your new lodgers will probably also enjoy reading your book and seeing what others have said before. You can often buy specially printed visitors' books; however, you can also use an ordinary exercise book, although as you may be using it for many years it is a good idea to have one with a hard cover. It should have columns for the visitor's name, date of departure or stay, address and comments. It is of course the comments which are the most interesting to read!

Post

If your lodger regularly receives a lot of post, you might suggest to him that he arranges for a postal redirect. If you are happy to forward his mail for him, make sure you get a forwarding address.

However, you will not want to act as an unpaid mail forwarding service forever, so make it clear that you will only do this for a limited time, and that any post you receive after that will be posted back marked 'return to sender'.

On the day that he departs

Make sure that his rent is paid up to date. If it is not, make sure that you get a payment from him before he leaves (although this will not always be possible).

It is often a good idea to go up and check his room before he goes, as it is surprising what people leave behind. Sometimes he will intend to leave things, but it is best to check before he leaves so that you save yourself the cost and bother of forwarding it to him by post.

Don't forget to check the bins also. I once had a Japanese student leave a book of American Express traveller's cheques in the bin!

Unpaid rent

In most cases your lodger will have paid rent up to the date that he goes. However, if he goes leaving rent outstanding, particularly if he is hard up or on a low income, you will probably never see it, and it is best to be realistic and accept from the start you are unlikely to be paid.

However, if you decide to give it a go, note that the only way you can force someone to pay if he refuses to pay voluntarily is by obtaining a County Court Judgement (CCJ) in the Small Claims Court. To do this you will need to have his current address for service of the court papers. For this reason if no other, it is a good idea to always get a forwarding address from your lodger before he departs.

There are debt collecting organisations around, but generally these prove to be expensive and are often ineffective, and if court proceedings are necessary they will need to do this through a solicitors' firm anyway, so you may end up paying two sets of fees. It is best to go direct to a firm of solicitors which specialise in debt collecting (you will find them in the Yellow Pages). However, it is not particularly difficult to bring a Court claim yourself, particularly if you have internet access and can use the Court's Money Claim Online service at www.moneyclaim.gov.uk.

You can also find guidance in Lawpack's *Small Claims Made Easy* or *The Quick Guide to Making a Money Claim Online* books and also on my website www.landlordlaw.co.uk.

Note, however, that there is little point in going to all the bother of obtaining a CCJ if your debtor does not have any money to pay it. The court enforcement procedures are not particularly effective, and it is as well to read up on this before you start. You will find some helpful leaflets on the enforcement of CCJs on the Court Service website at www.hmcourts-service.gov.uk.

After your lodger has gone

You will have your room back! It is nice to have lodgers but it is also often very nice when they go. However, if you need a lodger to pay the bills you will have to start the process of looking for another one.

If you are the one moving out

Note that your lodger will only have lodger status while you are living in the property and sharing accommodation. If you move out permanently, for example to go and work in another town, your lodger's status will then change to that of a tenant. As you will no longer be a resident landlord, the lodger will acquire an Assured Shorthold Tenancy (AST), from the time when you move out. It is best to accept this and get him to sign up a proper AST agreement at this time.

If you are looking to sell your property, you will need to ensure that the lodger has moved out first. It is unlikely that your purchasers will agree to sign and exchange contracts until this has been done.

And finally...

I hope you have found this book helpful, and now feel more confident in dealing with your lodgers. As mentioned above, in the vast majority of cases your lodgers will be entirely delightful and you will look back on your time with them with fond memories.

However, if you do encounter problems, the procedures set out in chapter 8 should help you deal with them.

Useful contacts

Some credit reference companies:

- Check my Tenant from Experian
  www.checkmytenant.co.uk

- Tenant Verify from LandlordZone
  www.tenantverify.co.uk

Energy Performance Certificates information:

- The Energy Saving Trust (EST)
  www.energysavingtrust.org.uk

- Landmark Information Group
  www.hcrregister.com

Other useful contacts:

- Communities and Local Government
  www.communities.gov.uk/housing

- The Gas Safe Register
  www.gassaferegister.co.uk
  or telephone 0800 408 5500

- The Heath and Safety Executive (HSE)
  www.hse.gov.uk

- Housing benefit/LHA resource centre
  www.dwp.gov.uk/local-authority-staff/housing-
  benefit/claims-processing/local-housing-allowance

- Landlord-Law (the author's site)
  www.landlordlaw.co.uk

- The Lodger Landlord (the author's site)
  www.lodgerlandlord.co.uk

- Money Claim Online
  www.moneyclaim.gov.uk

- The Statute Law Database
  www.statutelaw.gov.uk

- Trading Standards
  www.tradingstandards.gov.uk

- Unlock
  www.unlock.org.uk

Index